Bank Wisely

BY HEATHER E. SCHWARTZ

amicus
high interest

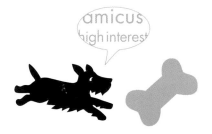

Amicus High Interest is published by Amicus
P.O. Box 1329, Mankato, MN 56002
www.amicuspublishing.us

Library of Congress Cataloging-in-Publication Data
Schwartz, Heather E.
 Bank wisely / by Heather E. Schwartz.
    pages cm. – (Money smarts)
Includes bibliographical references and index.
Audience: K to Grade 3.
Summary: "This photo-illustrated book for elementary readers
describes what a bank is, why to use a savings account,
and how checking accounts, loans, and credit cards work"–
Provided by publisher.
ISBN 978-1-60753-792-2 (library binding)
ISBN 978-1-60753-901-8 (ebook)
1. Bank accounts–Juvenile literature. 2. Banks and banking–
Juvenile literature. 3. Finance, Personal–Juvenile literature. I.
Title.
 HG1660.A3S38 2016
 332.1'7–dc23

                                       2014033262

Editor: Wendy Dieker
Series Designer: Kathleen Petelinsek
Book Designer: Aubrey Harper
Photo Researcher: Derek Brown

Photo Credits: Gallo Images - LKIS/Getty cover; JGI/
Jamie Grill/Blend Images/Corbis 5; Comstock Images /
Exactostock-1557/Superstock 6; Stewart Cohen/Pam Ostrow/
Blend Images/Corbis 8; Kate Kunz/Corbis 10-11; Jose Luis
Pelaez/Blend Images/Corbis 13; Image Source/Corbis 14;
Andresr/Shutterstock 17; Charlene Key/Shutterstock 18;
moodboard/Corbis 21; Don Mason/Corbis 22; CandyBox
Images/Shutterstock 25; Denisa Haldova/Corbis 26; 68/
Ocean/Corbis 28-29

Printed in Malaysia.

10 9 8 7 6 5 4 3 2 1

Table of Contents

Keep it in the Bank

Do you have some money? Where can you keep it? You could keep it in a piggy bank. You could hide it in a drawer. But what happens when your piggy bank is full? How can you keep track of all your money if it's in a drawer? It is wise to put your money in the bank.

A piggy bank is a good place to keep coins.

A banker will take your coins and put them in your account. Your money will be safe.

All About Accounts

Opening an **account** is a way to bank wisely. An account is an agreement with the bank. They keep your money safe. They also keep track of how much money you have.

A teller will help you. The tellers help **deposit** your money, or put it in your account. They also help you **withdraw** it. That means you take it out.

Banks keep track of the cash you put in your account.

 **Q** What if someone robs the bank?

The cash you put in the bank doesn't go in a special box just for you. It is put together with money from other customers. The bank keeps information about your money on a computer. That way, the bank will know how much money is yours.

Most banks are insured. That means you'll get your money back.

Do you want something big like a new bike? Or maybe a computer? You can use a savings account to save your money for big things. When your money is in the bank, it is not so easy to spend. You won't be as tempted to buy small things. It can feel good to save enough for something special.

This girl used a savings account to save money for a bike.

When you put your money in a savings account, the bank will use it. But you get something out of the deal, too. Free money! The bank pays you **interest** on the money in your savings account. The more you save, the more interest you earn.

 Why would the bank use my money?

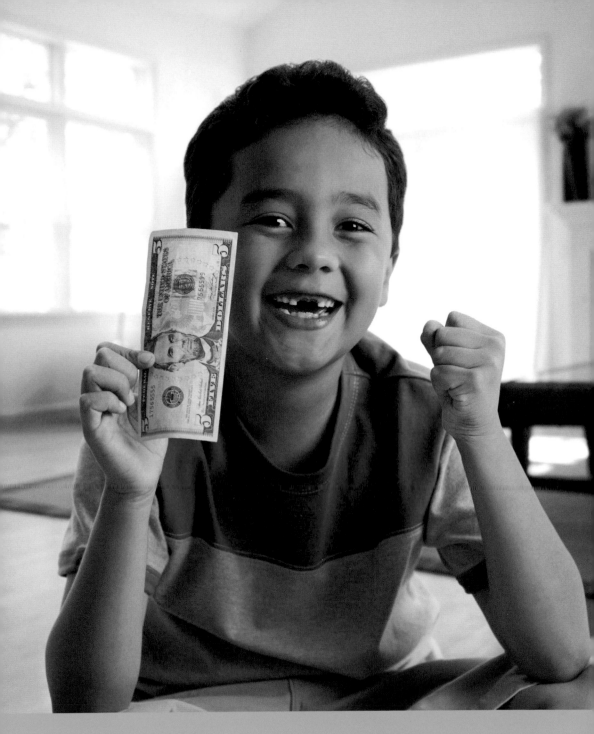

 It could be used to make **loans** to other customers. Even if they use it, the amount of money in your account won't change.

Check the statement from the bank to make sure there are no mistakes.

Banks will send you a **statement** every month. It will tell you how much money is in your account. You will see how much you put in and took out. Still, you should keep track of your money yourself, too. Then you can check for any mistakes.

Paper or Plastic?

When you take money out of your bank account, you leave with cash. You can spend it at the toy store, the bookstore, or wherever you like. But the bank lets people spend money in other ways, too. Have you ever seen your parents write a **check**? Or use a **debit card**? They're spending money from a bank account.

People use debit cards to
buy things at the store.

Writing a check is like asking
the bank to pay someone
with your money.

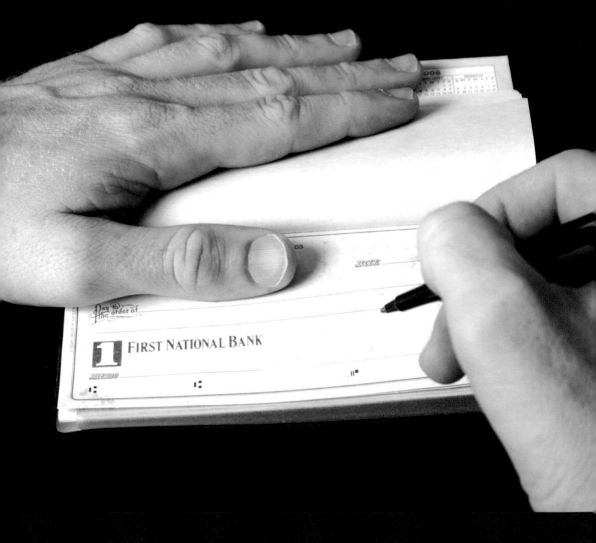

Q What if someone writes a check for more
money than he has in the bank?

When your dad writes a check, he fills in the name of the store he needs to pay. He also fills in the amount of money he owes. Then he signs the bottom of the check. A store worker takes the check to the bank. Then, the bank takes money out of your dad's bank account and gives it to the store.

 He will still owe the store money. Plus, he'll owe the bank and store extra fees.

Debit cards work the same way. A person might use a debit card to buy gas. He swipes it through a machine. It reads the card to make sure there's enough money in his account. If there is, the man gets his gasoline. The gas station gets money from his bank account.

This man is using a debit
card to buy gasoline.

**Banks give loans to people
so they can buy a house.**

Borrowing Money

Have you ever borrowed money from your parents? That was a loan. So where do your parents get loans? The bank! Loans help people buy things that cost a lot of money. Most people can't save enough to buy a house. It might take a lifetime! They don't wait to save up the money. They get a loan from the bank.

People can buy things right away when they use loans. But it's not free money. Banks charge interest. If you take out a loan, you have to pay back more than you borrowed. But you don't have to pay it all back at once. You make many small payments over time.

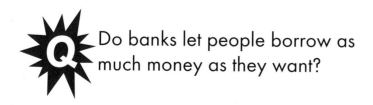
Do banks let people borrow as much money as they want?

Many people get loans
to buy a car. They make
payments to the bank.

 No, banks decide how much to lend.
People have to prove they can—
and will—pay the money back.

If you buy things online, you could use your parents' credit card. But get permission first!

Credit cards are another way to borrow money. People use them for smaller purchases. A credit card is just like other loans. The bank will charge interest to use the money. The interest can add up fast. It's wise to charge only what can be paid back right away.

The Bank and You

Can you use a bank wisely? You might not need a loan yet. But do you have a stuffed piggybank? Is your cash piling up? Maybe you want to open a savings account. Ask your parents to take you to the bank!

Bring your piggy bank to the bank!

Glossary

account An arrangement with the bank for them to keep your money safe.

check A piece of paper a person fills out to pay for something with money in a bank account.

credit card A card used to buy things; the credit card company sends the buyer a bill.

debit card A card used to buy things; the money comes right out of a person's checking account.

deposit To put money in an account.

interest A small bit of money the bank pays you for saving your money in an account.

loan An agreement with a bank to borrow money to buy something expensive; loans are paid back in small payments over time.

statement A list of all the money that was put in and taken out of an account and shows the current amount in the account.

withdraw To take money out of an account.

Read More

Brennan, Linda Crotta. *Banking*. North Mankato Minnesota: The Child's World, Inc., 2014.

Kawa, Katie. *My First Trip to the Bank*. New York: Gareth Stevens Publishing, 2012.

Manushkin, Fran. *Piggy Bank Problems*. North Mankato, Minnesota: Picture Window Books, 2013.

Websites

Banking Kids Elementary
www.bankingkids.com/pages/elem.html

Hands On Banking
www.handsonbanking.org/htdocs/en/k/

The Mint: How Banks Work
www.themint.org/kids/how-banks-work.html

Every effort has been made to ensure that these websites are appropriate for children. However, because of the nature of the Internet, it is impossible to guarantee that these sites will remain active indefinitely or that their contents will not be altered.

Index

About the Author